NEW YORK FOREVER

Dr. Maxwell Shimba

TABLE OF CONTENTS

PREFACE

New York City, a sprawling metropolis brimming with life, serves as the dynamic backdrop for this tale of friendship, ambition, and the relentless pursuit of dreams. In the pages that follow, you will meet three individuals—Emma, Daniel, and Maria—whose lives intertwine in unexpected ways, each driven by their unique passions yet united by their shared love for the city that never sleeps.

Emma, a talented journalist, finds herself navigating the complexities of storytelling in a world that craves authenticity. Her "Hidden Gems" series uncovers the untold stories of ordinary people, revealing the extraordinary within the everyday. Through her lens, we see the beauty and resilience that define New York, and later, the world.

Daniel, an architect with a vision for sustainable urban living, confronts the challenges of turning his dreams into reality. His projects, which aim to blend ecological consciousness with community engagement, take him from the heart of Brooklyn to the innovative landscapes of

Singapore. Daniel's journey is one of perseverance, creativity, and the constant quest for balance between ambition and practicality.

Maria, an artist and community organizer, champions the transformative power of art. Her "Art for All" initiative seeks to democratize creativity, bringing it to underserved communities and fostering a sense of belonging and expression. Her story is a testament to the power of passion, the importance of giving back, and the profound impact of nurturing the human spirit through artistic endeavors.

As their paths unfold, Emma, Daniel, and Maria encounter a series of serendipitous events that challenge and inspire them. From unexpected collaborations to unforeseen obstacles, their experiences highlight the unpredictability of life and the importance of resilience and adaptability.

This novel, the first volume in the "New York Forever" series, delves into the essence of what it means to dream big in a city known for its relentless pace and boundless opportunities. It explores themes of friendship, love, sacrifice, and the unyielding pursuit of one's calling. Through the highs and lows, triumphs and setbacks, the bond between these three friends remains a constant source of strength and inspiration.

"New York Forever" is more than just a story about a city and its inhabitants; it is a celebration of the human spirit and the connections that sustain us. Whether you are a lifelong New Yorker or someone who dreams of experiencing the city's magic, this book invites you to walk alongside Emma, Daniel, and Maria as they navigate their way through the labyrinth of life, love, and ambition.

Welcome to their world. Welcome to New York Forever.

viii

DR. MAXWELL SHIMBA

CHAPTER 01

THE CITY THAT NEVER SLEEPS

New York City never slept. The streets buzzed with a symphony of sounds – honking taxis, chattering pedestrians, and the distant rumble of the subway. Skyscrapers loomed overhead, their windows gleaming with the promise of a million untold stories.

Amidst the chaos, Emma Sullivan navigated her way through the crowded sidewalk with practiced ease. She was a writer, always in search of the next great story, her eyes constantly scanning the faces of strangers for a hint of inspiration. Emma had moved to New York two years ago, leaving behind a quiet life in the Midwest for the electrifying pulse of the city.

On the other side of town, Daniel Carter was making his morning coffee in his small but stylish apartment. A successful architect, Daniel had an eye for detail and a passion for design that had landed him a job at one of the top firms in Manhattan. He loved the city's energy, but there was always a part of him that felt something was missing.

Meanwhile, in a cozy café in Greenwich Village, Maria Rodriguez was setting up for another busy day. Maria owned the café, a dream she had nurtured since her days working as a barista during college. Her café was a haven for artists, writers, and dreamers – a place where creativity flourished over cups of steaming coffee.

Each of them was immersed in their world, unaware that their lives were on a collision course that would change everything.

As the day unfolded, Emma found herself drawn to a small park near her apartment. She often came here to think, the tranquility of the trees and the laughter of children providing a perfect backdrop for her thoughts. Today, however, she was distracted by a man sketching on a bench.

Daniel was lost in his work, sketching the park's landscape with precise, fluid strokes. He looked up just as Emma approached, their eyes meeting in a moment of mutual curiosity.

"Mind if I sit?" Emma asked, gesturing to the empty spot beside him.

"Not at all," Daniel replied, shifting his sketchpad slightly. "I'm Daniel, by the way."

"Emma," she said with a smile. "What are you drawing?"

"Just the park," he said, showing her the intricate lines and shading of his sketch. "It's my way of capturing the city's beauty."

Emma nodded, admiring his work. "It's amazing. You have a real talent."

"Thanks," Daniel said, his cheeks flushing slightly. "What about you? What do you do?"

"I'm a writer," Emma said. "Always looking for inspiration."

They talked for a while longer, discovering common interests and sharing stories of their lives in the city. As they parted ways, both felt a spark of something new and exciting.

That evening, as Maria was closing up the café, she found herself thinking about her own dreams and ambitions.

She had built a life she loved, but there was always a part of her that wondered what else was out there.

The city that never sleeps had a way of bringing people together, weaving their stories into the vibrant tapestry of New York. As the night descended and the lights of the city twinkled like stars, Emma, Daniel, and Maria went to bed with a sense of anticipation, knowing that in a city like New York, anything was possible.

CHAPTER 02

DREAMS AND AMBITIONS

The morning sun cast a golden hue over New York City, waking it from its brief slumber. Emma Sullivan, fresh from her encounter with Daniel, felt a renewed sense of purpose. She sat at her cluttered desk in her small apartment, fingers poised over her laptop keyboard. Her mind was abuzz with ideas, each one vying for her attention.

Emma's dreams were vast and ambitious. She wanted to write a novel that would capture the essence of the city – its vibrancy, its struggles, its triumphs. But more than that, she wanted to tell stories that resonated with people, stories that would make them feel understood and seen. As she typed the first lines of her new manuscript, she felt the familiar rush of excitement that always accompanied the start of a new project.

Across the city, Daniel Carter was already at work, the blueprints for a new skyscraper spread out before him. His office, perched high above the bustling streets, offered a panoramic view of Manhattan. To Daniel, each building was more than just a structure; it was a testament to human ingenuity and ambition. His latest project was a sleek, modern tower that would redefine the skyline.

Daniel's ambition was to leave a lasting legacy through his designs. He wanted to create spaces that inspired awe and fostered community. As he sketched out the final details, he thought about his chance meeting with Emma. There was something about her – her passion, her curiosity – that intrigued him. It was a reminder that even in a city as vast as New York, connections could be made in the most unexpected ways.

Meanwhile, Maria Rodriguez was busy with the morning rush at her café. The aroma of freshly brewed coffee filled the air as customers lined up for their daily fix. Maria moved with practiced efficiency, greeting regulars by name and making sure everything ran smoothly. Her café was more than just a business; it was her sanctuary, a place where she could express her creativity and bring people together.

Maria's dream was to expand her café into a chain that would retain its unique charm and personal touch. She wanted to create spaces where people could feel at home, no matter where they were. As she looked out at the bustling crowd, she felt a surge of pride and determination. She was building something special, one cup of coffee at a time.

As the day wore on, Emma, Daniel, and Maria each faced their own challenges. Emma struggled with writer's block, staring at the blinking cursor on her screen in frustration. Daniel hit a snag in his design, a structural issue that threatened to derail his project. Maria dealt with an unexpected equipment failure, throwing her carefully planned schedule into chaos.

But each of them pushed through, driven by their dreams and ambitions. Emma took a walk through her neighborhood, letting the sights and sounds of the city spark her creativity. Daniel sought advice from a trusted colleague, finding a solution to his problem. Maria improvised, using her resourcefulness to keep the café running smoothly.

That evening, as the city settled into its nighttime rhythm, Emma found herself at Maria's café. She had discovered it by chance, drawn in by the warm, inviting atmosphere. As she sipped her coffee, she felt a sense of contentment. The café was a microcosm of the city – vibrant, diverse, full of life.

Daniel, too, found himself drawn to the café. He spotted Emma at a corner table, engrossed in her writing. He hesitated for a moment before approaching her.

"Mind if I join you?" he asked, holding his coffee.

Emma looked up, a smile spreading across her face. "Of course not. It's good to see you again."

They talked late into the evening, sharing their dreams and ambitions. Maria watched them from behind the counter, a knowing smile on her face. She had seen many such encounters in her café, each one a reminder of the city's magic.

As they parted ways, Emma and Daniel felt a sense of possibility. They were dreamers in a city of dreams, and their paths had crossed for a reason. New York had a way of bringing people together, of weaving their stories into its grand tapestry.

In their own ways, they were all chasing something – a dream, an ambition, a connection. And in the city that never sleeps, anything was possible.

CHAPTER 03

CROSSING PATHS

The days turned into weeks, and the city's rhythm continued unabated. Emma, Daniel, and Maria found themselves increasingly drawn to one another's company. Their lives, previously marked by solitude and single-minded pursuit of their goals, began to intersect in ways they hadn't anticipated.

Emma had made the café her regular writing spot. The vibrant energy, coupled with the comforting aroma of freshly brewed coffee, seemed to banish her writer's block. She often found Daniel there, sketching designs or reviewing blueprints. Their conversations flowed easily, an effortless blend of professional ambition and personal curiosity.

One evening, as Emma packed up her laptop, Daniel caught her eye. "There's an art exhibit opening this weekend at the Met," he said. "I was thinking of going. Would you like to join me?"

Emma's eyes lit up. "I'd love to. It sounds amazing."

The night of the exhibit, the Met was alive with the buzz of art enthusiasts and critics. Emma and Daniel wandered through the galleries, losing themselves in the vibrant colors and intricate details of the artworks. Each piece told a story, and as they discussed their interpretations, they found their connection deepening.

Meanwhile, Maria was dealing with her own set of challenges. The equipment failure at the café had turned out to be more serious than she'd initially thought, and she was struggling to keep up with repairs. One afternoon, as she juggled phone calls and customer orders, Daniel walked in.

Seeing her distress, he approached. "Is everything okay?"

Maria sighed, wiping her brow. "Just dealing with some equipment issues. It's been a nightmare trying to get everything fixed."

Daniel frowned, thinking. "I have a friend who's an engineer. He might be able to help. Would you like me to ask him to take a look?"

Maria's face brightened with relief. "That would be amazing. Thank you, Daniel."

True to his word, Daniel's friend arrived the next day and swiftly diagnosed the problem, getting the café back on track. Maria was immensely grateful, and her friendship with Daniel grew stronger.

As the weeks passed, the trio began to spend more time together outside the café. They explored the city's hidden gems – quaint bookstores, eclectic galleries, and charming street markets. They shared their stories and dreams, finding support and encouragement in one another.

One crisp autumn evening, the three of them found themselves at a rooftop bar, gazing out over the glittering skyline. The view was breathtaking, the city a sea of lights stretching into the horizon.

"Sometimes I forget how beautiful this city is," Emma mused, her voice soft.

"It has a way of surprising you," Daniel agreed. "No matter how long you've been here."

Maria raised her glass. "To new beginnings and unexpected friendships."

They clinked their glasses, the sound a delicate chime against the backdrop of the city. In that moment, they felt an unspoken bond, a sense of belonging that transcended their individual ambitions.

The following week, Emma received an email from a prestigious literary magazine. Her short story, inspired by her experiences in New York and the people she'd met, had been accepted for publication. Overwhelmed with joy, she immediately called Daniel and Maria to share the news.

"That's incredible, Emma!" Daniel exclaimed. "You deserve it."

Maria's eyes sparkled with pride. "We need to celebrate. How about dinner at my place?"

That night, Maria's apartment was filled with laughter and the rich aromas of home-cooked food. They toasted to Emma's success, their camaraderie a testament to the city's ability to forge unexpected connections.

As the evening drew to a close, Emma looked around at her friends, feeling a profound sense of gratitude. New York had given her more than she'd ever imagined – not just a place to pursue her dreams, but people who understood and supported her.

In the city that never sleeps, their paths had crossed for a reason. And as they faced the future, they knew they were no longer alone. They were a part of something bigger, a tapestry of dreams and ambitions, woven together by the magic of New York.

CHAPTER 04

A NEW BEGINNING

The winter chill settled over New York City, blanketing the streets in a crisp, invigorating cold. Emma, Daniel, and Maria had found a comfortable rhythm in their intertwined lives, supporting each other's pursuits while nurturing their own dreams. As the holiday season approached, the city's energy shifted, becoming even more vibrant and alive with possibility.

Emma's short story publication had opened new doors for her. She received an invitation to speak at a local writer's conference, an opportunity she knew could propel her career forward. Nervous but excited, she turned to her friends for support.

"Do you think I can do this?" Emma asked one evening, seated in Maria's cozy apartment, a mug of hot cocoa warming her hands.

"Absolutely," Daniel said without hesitation. "You have a unique voice, Emma. People need to hear it."

Maria nodded in agreement. "You've already come so far. This is just the beginning."

Encouraged by their confidence, Emma threw herself into preparing her speech. She spent countless hours drafting and revising, wanting to ensure she conveyed her journey and the lessons she'd learned along the way. When the day of the conference arrived, she stood before the audience, her heart pounding with anticipation.

As she began to speak, the initial nerves gave way to a calm determination. She spoke of her move to New York, the struggles she faced, and the serendipitous encounters that had shaped her path. Her words resonated with the audience, drawing nods of understanding and applause of appreciation.

Afterward, several attendees approached her, sharing how her story had inspired them. Emma felt a deep sense of fulfillment, knowing that her words had made a difference. As she left the conference, she spotted Daniel and Maria waiting for her, their faces beaming with pride.

"You were amazing!" Maria exclaimed, hugging her tightly.

Daniel nodded, a warm smile on his face. "We knew you could do it."

Meanwhile, Daniel was facing a new beginning of his own. His innovative skyscraper design had garnered significant attention, leading to an offer to lead a major project in Dubai. It was an opportunity of a lifetime, but it also meant leaving New York for several months.

Over dinner one evening, he shared the news with Emma and Maria. "I've been offered a project in Dubai," he said, his voice tinged with excitement and uncertainty. "It's a huge opportunity, but it means I'll be away for a while."

Emma's eyes widened. "Daniel, that's incredible! You have to take it."

Maria nodded in agreement. "This is your dream, Daniel. We'll miss you, but we'll be here when you get back."

Their unwavering support bolstered his resolve. As he prepared for the move, he made sure to spend as much time as possible with his friends, cherishing the moments they had together. The night before his departure, they gathered at their favorite rooftop bar, the city lights sparkling around them.

"To new beginnings," Daniel said, raising his glass.

"To chasing dreams," Emma added, clinking her glass with his.

"And to the friendships that keep us grounded," Maria concluded, her voice filled with warmth.

As they toasted, Daniel felt a sense of peace. He knew that no matter where his journey took him, he had found a family in the city he loved.

Maria, too, was on the cusp of a new beginning. Inspired by Emma's success and Daniel's bold leap, she decided to expand her café. She found a perfect location for a second branch, envisioning a space that would retain the charm and intimacy of her original café while reaching a broader audience.

She confided in Emma and Daniel about her plans, their encouragement fueling her determination. With their support and her own unwavering drive, she navigated the complexities of opening a new location. There were challenges, but Maria faced them head-on, driven by her vision and the community she had built.

The grand opening of the new café was a resounding success. Customers flocked to the new location, drawn by the warmth and creativity that Maria infused into every corner. As she looked around at the bustling space, she felt a surge of pride and gratitude.

Emma, Daniel, and Maria each faced their new beginnings with courage and optimism, knowing that their paths were forever intertwined. In the heart of New York City, they had found not only their dreams but each other. And as they continued to chase their ambitions, they knew they had the strength of their friendship to guide them through whatever lay ahead.

CHAPTER 05

UNEXPECTED CONNECTIONS

With the new year, the trio found themselves facing their new beginnings with renewed vigor and determination. The city, ever-changing and dynamic, seemed to reflect their own transformations.

Daniel's move to Dubai had been bittersweet. Though excited about the project, he missed the familiar sights and sounds of New York and, most of all, his friends. The new city was a marvel, an architectural dreamscape, and his work was challenging and fulfilling. Yet, in the quiet moments, he found himself longing for the camaraderie he had shared with Emma and Maria.

One evening, as he sat on his balcony overlooking Dubai's glittering skyline, he received a video call from Emma. Her face lit up his screen, and seeing her smile brought a wave of warmth.

"How's the desert treating you?" Emma asked, her voice cheerful despite the distance.

"It's amazing, but I miss you guys," Daniel admitted. "How are things back in New York?"

Emma updated him on her writing projects, Maria's new café, and the little adventures they had been having. "We're planning to visit you once your project is completed," she added. "Maria and I have already started saving up."

Daniel's heart swelled with gratitude. "I can't wait. It'll be great to show you around."

Back in New York, Emma was thriving. Her success at the writer's conference had opened up several opportunities, including a book deal. She found herself working tirelessly on her manuscript, pouring her heart and soul into every chapter. Despite the long hours, she felt more alive than ever.

Maria's new café had quickly become a beloved neighborhood spot, and she was busier than ever managing both locations. One afternoon, as she was rushing between the two cafés, she bumped into a young woman who was struggling to carry a stack of art supplies.

"Here, let me help you with that," Maria offered, grabbing some of the items before they could tumble to the ground.

"Thank you so much," the woman said, her face flushed with gratitude. "I'm Isabella, by the way. Just moved to the city for an art residency."

Maria introduced herself, and as they walked together, she learned that Isabella was a talented painter who had been awarded a prestigious grant to study and create in New York. She invited Isabella to visit her café, offering it as a space for inspiration and relaxation.

Isabella took her up on the offer and soon became a regular at the café. She and Maria struck up a friendship, bonded by their shared passion for creativity and their journeys as women building their dreams in the city.

Meanwhile, Emma found herself drawn to a new project. She had always been fascinated by the stories of the people she encountered daily, and she decided to start a series of interviews and profiles focusing on New York's diverse residents. Her first subject was a street musician she often saw near Central Park.

His name was Jamal, and his soulful saxophone playing had captivated Emma on numerous occasions. She approached him one chilly afternoon, introducing herself and explaining her project. Jamal was intrigued and agreed to be interviewed.

As they talked, Emma learned about Jamal's journey — his struggles, his triumphs, and his love for music that had seen him through the toughest times. His story was both heartbreaking and inspiring, a testament to the resilience and spirit of New Yorkers.

Emma's series, which she titled "City Souls," quickly gained traction. Readers were moved by the raw, honest accounts of the people who made up the fabric of New York. Each profile brought her closer to the city she loved, deepening her understanding and appreciation of its unique vibrancy.

As winter melted into spring, the unexpected connections each of them made began to intertwine, creating a richer, more colorful tapestry. Maria hosted an art show at her café, featuring Isabella's work, and it was a resounding success. Emma's profiles were turning into a book, a celebration of the city's indomitable spirit.

One evening, as Emma and Maria sat in the café, sipping their drinks and discussing their plans, Daniel's face appeared on Emma's phone screen.

"Guess what?" he said, his voice bubbling with excitement. "I'm coming back to New York next month! The project wrapped up ahead of schedule."

Emma and Maria cheered, their faces alight with joy. "We can't wait to have you back!" Maria exclaimed.

The three friends, though separated by distance, remained connected through their shared experiences and the city that had brought them together. They knew that no matter where life took them, their bond was unbreakable.

And as they looked forward to Daniel's return, they also looked forward to the new adventures and connections that awaited them in the ever-surprising, ever-changing city of New York.

CHAPTER 06

REUNIONS AND REVELATIONS

The air in New York buzzed with anticipation as the date of Daniel's return approached. Emma and Maria had planned a welcome-back party at Maria's café, inviting their new friends and the regulars who had become part of their extended family.

The night of Daniel's arrival was one of those perfect spring evenings, with the city wrapped in a gentle warmth and the scent of blooming flowers in the air. Emma and Maria were bustling around the café, putting the finishing touches on the decorations and food. Isabella had offered to create a mural for the occasion, and her vibrant artwork now adorned one wall, capturing the spirit of the city and their friendship.

As the guests began to arrive, the café filled with laughter and chatter. Jamal, the street musician, played his saxophone in a corner, adding a soulful melody to the festive atmosphere. Emma checked her phone for the umpteenth time, her excitement barely contained.

Finally, the door opened, and Daniel walked in. The room erupted in cheers and applause as he was enveloped in hugs and warm greetings. He looked around, taking in the familiar faces and the new ones, his heart swelling with joy.

"I missed you guys so much," Daniel said, his voice thick with emotion.

Emma and Maria beamed at him. "Welcome home," Maria said, handing him a drink. "This place wasn't the same without you."

As the evening wore on, Daniel shared stories from his time in Dubai, his eyes sparkling with excitement as he described the innovative designs and the cultural experiences he had encountered. Emma and Maria updated him on their projects, their successes, and the new friendships they had forged in his absence.

Later, as the party wound down, the three friends found themselves sitting on the rooftop terrace, gazing out over the city. The lights twinkled like stars, casting a magical glow over the scene.

"I've been thinking a lot about the future," Daniel said, breaking the comfortable silence. "Dubai was incredible, but New York is where my heart is. I want to start my own architectural firm here, focus on projects that give back to the community."

Emma and Maria exchanged glances, their eyes shining with pride and excitement. "That's amazing, Daniel," Emma said. "You've always had such a passion for this city. You're going to do great things."

Maria nodded. "And we'll be here to support you every step of the way."

Inspired by Daniel's vision, Emma also shared her latest idea. "I want to expand 'City Souls' into a full-fledged multimedia project," she said. "Podcasts, videos, maybe even a documentary. There are so many stories out there waiting to be told."

"That sounds incredible, Emma," Daniel said, his admiration clear. "You have such a gift for capturing the essence of this city and its people."

Maria, too, had been contemplating her next steps. "I've been thinking about opening a community center," she said. "A place where people can come together, learn new skills, and find support. I've seen how much good a sense of community can do, and I want to create more spaces for that."

Emma and Daniel were immediately supportive. "That's a fantastic idea, Maria," Emma said. "You've already created such a welcoming environment with your cafés. A community center would be an extension of that."

As they sat together, sharing their dreams and plans, they realized how much they had grown since their paths had first crossed. Their individual journeys had strengthened their bond, each of them inspiring and supporting the others in ways they had never imagined.

In the days that followed, they threw themselves into their new projects with renewed energy. Daniel began laying the groundwork for his architectural firm, reaching out to contacts and securing funding. Emma started recording interviews and scouting locations for her multimedia project, while Maria began organizing community meetings to gather input and support for her center.

Their paths continued to intertwine, each of them contributing to the others' successes. Isabella's art became a central feature in Emma's documentary, her vibrant murals capturing the stories and spirit of the city. Jamal's music provided the soundtrack, his soulful melodies weaving through the narrative.

The trio's friendship was the heart of their endeavors, a source of strength and inspiration. They knew that whatever challenges lay ahead, they could face them together.

And in the ever-changing, ever-surprising city of New York, their stories were just beginning.

CHAPTER 07

THE HEART OF THE CITY

With spring in full bloom, New York City seemed to embrace the sense of renewal and possibility that Emma, Daniel, and Maria felt in their lives. Their new projects were underway, and the energy of their dreams seemed to infuse the city around them.

Emma's "City Souls" project had quickly gained momentum. Her profiles of everyday New Yorkers were being read and shared widely, drawing attention from local media and even a few national outlets. Inspired by the response, she began hosting live events at Maria's cafés, where she would interview her subjects in front of an audience.

One evening, as the café filled with patrons eager to hear the latest story, Emma prepared to interview a subway performer named Lina, whose hauntingly beautiful voice had captivated commuters for years. Daniel and Maria were there, as always, ready to support their friend.

Lina's story was one of resilience and passion. She had come to New York from a small town, chasing her dream of becoming a singer. Despite countless rejections and hardships, she had found a home in the city's subway system, where her voice resonated with the hopes and struggles of its people.

As Lina sang one of her original songs, the café fell silent, the only sound the haunting melody weaving through the air. Emma watched the audience, seeing the impact of Lina's story reflected in their faces. This was why she did what she did – to give a voice to those who might otherwise go unheard.

After the event, as they helped clean up the café, Emma turned to Daniel and Maria. "I think we should take 'City Souls' on the road," she said. "There are so many stories across the city, in every borough and neighborhood. I want to capture them all."

Daniel and Maria exchanged excited glances. "That sounds amazing," Daniel said. "We can help with logistics and planning."

"And I can host events at both cafés," Maria added. "Make them community hubs where people can come together to share their stories."

Inspired by Emma's vision, they began to map out a plan for a series of events across the city. They reached out to community centers, libraries, and local businesses, finding enthusiastic partners eager to support their project.

Meanwhile, Daniel was making strides with his architectural firm. He had secured his first major project – a community housing development in Brooklyn. It was a dream come true, a chance to create something that would have a lasting impact on the city he loved.

One afternoon, as he walked the site with his team, he felt a deep sense of fulfillment. This was why he had become an architect – to build not just structures, but communities. He could see the future taking shape before his eyes, a vibrant, welcoming space that would provide homes and hope for countless families.

Back at the café, Maria was deep into her own project. The plans for her community center were coming together, and she had secured a location in a historic building in Harlem. She spent her days meeting with architects, community leaders, and potential donors, driven by her vision of a space where people could come together to learn, grow, and support one another.

One evening, as Emma and Daniel joined her at the new site, they could feel the potential of the space. The old building had a rich history, and Maria's plans would honor that legacy while creating something new and vital.

"This place is going to be incredible," Emma said, looking around at the high ceilings and wide, welcoming rooms.

"I can already see it," Daniel agreed. "You're going to make such a difference here, Maria."

As the three friends stood together, imagining the future, they felt a profound sense of connection – to each other, to the city, and to the dreams that had brought them together.

The grand opening of Maria's second café had drawn a large crowd, and she had quickly become a beloved fixture in the community. Her warmth and generosity had created a space where people felt at home, and she was determined to replicate that success with her community center.

As they continued to work on their projects, they faced challenges and setbacks, but their shared support and friendship kept them going. They knew that together, they could overcome anything.

One sunny afternoon, as they sat in the park, enjoying a rare moment of relaxation, Emma looked around at her friends and felt a deep sense of gratitude. "We've come a long way, haven't we?" she said, her voice filled with wonder.

Daniel nodded. "And we've still got a long way to go."

Maria smiled, her eyes sparkling with determination. "But we'll get there. Together."

In the heart of New York City, their stories were just beginning. They had found not only their dreams but a family – one that would support and inspire them through whatever lay ahead.

And as the city continued to change and grow, they knew they would be right there with it, building their futures and the future of the city they loved.

CHAPTER 08

NEW HORIZONS

The summer heat settled over New York, bringing with it a sense of vibrancy and endless possibility. Emma, Daniel, and Maria had found their rhythm, each deeply immersed in their respective projects while always making time to support one another.

Emma's "City Souls" project was in full swing, with events planned in all five boroughs. The stories she uncovered were as diverse as the city itself, each one a testament to the resilience and spirit of its inhabitants. She had started working on a documentary, capturing the faces and voices of those she interviewed, with Isabella's artwork providing a visual backdrop to the narratives.

One afternoon, Emma found herself in the Bronx, preparing for an interview with a community organizer named

Marcus. He had spent decades advocating for better housing and education in his neighborhood, and his passion for his work was palpable. As they sat in a small park, surrounded by children playing and neighbors chatting, Marcus shared his journey.

"I've seen this neighborhood go through a lot of changes," Marcus said, his eyes thoughtful. "But the one thing that's never changed is the strength of the people here. They fight for their community, for their families. That's what keeps me going."

Emma listened intently, her heart swelling with admiration. These were the stories that needed to be told, the voices that deserved to be heard. As she wrapped up the interview, she felt a renewed sense of purpose.

Meanwhile, Daniel's architectural firm was making significant progress on the community housing project in Brooklyn. The construction site was a hive of activity, with workers and architects bustling about, bringing Daniel's vision to life. He spent long hours on-site, ensuring every detail was perfect.

One evening, as the sun set over the city, Daniel stood on the rooftop of a nearly completed building, looking out over the skyline. He could see the future residents moving in, families finding a home and a community in the spaces he had designed. It was a dream come true, a culmination of years of hard work and dedication.

As he gazed out over the city, his phone buzzed with a message from Emma. "We're meeting at Maria's tonight," it read. "Can't wait to hear all about your project!"

Smiling, Daniel made his way to the café, eager to share his progress with his friends. When he arrived, the familiar warmth and chatter of the café enveloped him, and he spotted Emma and Maria at their usual table, deep in conversation.

"Hey, you two," Daniel greeted, sliding into a seat. "What's the latest?"

Emma beamed. "I just finished an incredible interview in the Bronx. Marcus is a real inspiration. I can't wait for you to see the footage."

Maria nodded. "And I've got some exciting news too. We've secured enough funding to start renovations on the community center! Construction starts next month."

Daniel's eyes lit up with pride and excitement. "That's amazing, Maria! I knew you could do it."

As they shared updates and plans, their conversation flowed effortlessly, each of them buoyed by the others' successes. They were a team, each contributing their unique talents and perspectives to the collective dream they were building.

One night, as they sat on the rooftop terrace, looking out over the city, Emma brought up an idea that had been percolating in her mind. "What if we collaborated on a project?" she suggested. "Something that combines our skills and passions, and makes a real impact on the city."

Daniel and Maria exchanged intrigued glances. "What do you have in mind?" Maria asked.

Emma took a deep breath. "I've been thinking about creating a multimedia exhibit, something that showcases the stories I've been collecting, along with Daniel's architectural designs and Maria's community initiatives. A celebration of New York's spirit and resilience."

Daniel's eyes widened with excitement. "That sounds incredible. We could create an immersive experience, with interactive displays and virtual reality tours of the housing projects."

Maria nodded enthusiastically. "And we could host workshops and events at the community center, bringing people together to share their own stories and ideas."

As they brainstormed, their vision began to take shape, a project that would bring together their passions and talents in a way that celebrated the city they loved. They knew it would be a massive undertaking, but they were ready for the challenge.

With their new collaborative project on the horizon, the trio threw themselves into the planning and preparation. They reached out to partners and sponsors, secured a venue, and began designing the exhibits. The city, ever vibrant and full of possibility, seemed to respond to their energy, opening doors and creating opportunities at every turn.

As they worked together, their bond grew even stronger, each of them inspired by the others' dedication and creativity. They were more than friends; they were a team, a family, united by their love for New York and their determination to make a difference.

The summer flew by in a whirlwind of activity and excitement, and as autumn approached, they knew they were on the cusp of something extraordinary. Their project, a celebration of the city's heart and soul, was coming to life, and they couldn't wait to share it with the world.

CHAPTER 09

BRINGING IT ALL TOGETHER

Autumn in New York brought a crispness to the air and a sense of urgency to the trio's work. The multimedia exhibit, which they had decided to call "New York Stories: The Heartbeat of a City," was set to open in December. The pressure was on to finalize details and ensure everything came together seamlessly.

Emma spent her days editing interviews and coordinating with Isabella on the visual elements. The café transformed into an impromptu studio where they reviewed footage and discussed artistic concepts. Isabella's murals and portraits brought a vibrant, emotional layer to the stories Emma had captured, creating a powerful visual narrative.

Daniel was deep in the technical aspects, designing the interactive displays and virtual reality tours that would give visitors an immersive experience. His architectural expertise was crucial in creating a layout that guided visitors through the exhibit, ensuring they felt connected to the stories being told. Late nights were spent fine-tuning digital models and coordinating with tech teams.

Maria juggled the final preparations for her community center with her role in the exhibit. Her experience in event planning and her network of community contacts were invaluable. She organized workshops, panel discussions, and community events that would complement the exhibit, ensuring it was not just a display but a dynamic, engaging experience.

One chilly November evening, as they gathered in Maria's newly renovated community center, they reviewed their progress. The center itself was a testament to Maria's dedication, with welcoming spaces for classes, meetings, and events. The walls were adorned with artwork from local artists, creating a warm and inspiring atmosphere.

"We're almost there," Emma said, looking around at her friends. "I can't believe how far we've come."

Daniel nodded, exhaustion and excitement evident in his eyes. "It's going to be amazing. We just need to keep pushing."

Maria smiled, her face glowing with pride. "This is what we've been working for. We're making a real difference."

As the opening day approached, the city buzzed with anticipation. Word of the exhibit had spread, and tickets were selling fast. Media outlets picked up the story, intrigued by the unique blend of personal narratives, art, and technology.

The night before the opening, the trio gathered one last time to walk through the exhibit. The space was transformed into a journey through New York's diverse communities, with each section highlighting different stories and themes. Interactive displays allowed visitors to explore Daniel's architectural projects and the stories of the people who would live there. Maria's community initiatives were featured prominently, showcasing the impact of grassroots efforts in creating positive change.

In the center of the exhibit, a large screen played Emma's documentary, interspersed with live performances from musicians like Jamal and street artists who brought the city's sounds and sights to life. Isabella's artwork tied everything together, providing a vivid, emotional backdrop that captured the essence of the city.

As they stood in the center of the exhibit, taking it all in, Daniel spoke. "We did it. We really did it."

Emma nodded, tears of pride and joy in her eyes. "This is just the beginning. There are so many more stories to tell."

Maria hugged them both, her heart full. "We've created something special. And we've done it together."

The opening night was a resounding success. Visitors moved through the exhibit with awe and appreciation, engaging with the stories and experiences on display. Media coverage was overwhelmingly positive, praising the innovative blend of art, technology, and community engagement.

Emma, Daniel, and Maria spent the evening mingling with guests, sharing their journey and vision. As they moved through the crowd, they could feel the energy and excitement, the sense of connection and community that had driven them from the start.

In the weeks that followed, the exhibit continued to draw large crowds, sparking conversations and inspiring new projects. Emma received numerous invitations to speak and collaborate, while Daniel's firm gained new clients interested in his community-focused approach. Maria's community center flourished, becoming a hub for creativity and support.

As the exhibit drew to a close, the trio reflected on what they had accomplished. They had not only achieved their dreams but had created a lasting impact on the city they loved. Their friendship had deepened, their bond strengthened by the challenges they had faced and the successes they had shared.

One evening, as they sat together on the rooftop terrace, looking out over the city, they felt a profound sense of gratitude and purpose. They knew there were still many stories to tell, many dreams to pursue, and they were ready for whatever came next.

Emma raised her glass, a smile playing on her lips. "To New York, and to us. May we always find new stories and new adventures."

Daniel and Maria clinked their glasses with hers, their hearts full of hope and excitement.

"To New York," Daniel echoed. "And to us."

15

CHAPTER 10

NEW BEGINNINGS

With the success of "New York Stories: The Heartbeat of a City" still fresh, Emma, Daniel, and Maria found themselves at the cusp of new beginnings. The exhibit had not only brought their work into the spotlight but also opened up new opportunities that they were eager to explore.

Emma's multimedia project had gained significant attention. She was approached by a publishing house interested in turning "City Souls" into a book. Thrilled by the prospect, she began working on a manuscript, compiling the most compelling stories she had collected over the years. Her interviews would be accompanied by Isabella's artwork, creating a visually stunning and emotionally resonant narrative.

One afternoon, as she sat in a cozy corner of Maria's café, Emma worked on the book's introduction. The café's familiar buzz provided the perfect backdrop as she reflected on the journey that had led her here.

Meanwhile, Daniel's architectural firm was thriving. The Brooklyn housing project had become a model for sustainable, community-focused development, attracting attention from city planners and developers alike. Daniel found himself invited to speak at conferences and participate in panels on urban development and social impact.

One morning, as he reviewed blueprints in his office, Daniel received an email that caught his attention. It was an invitation from a prestigious architecture firm in Europe, interested in collaborating on a large-scale urban renewal project. The opportunity was tempting, promising new challenges and international recognition.

That evening, he shared the news with Emma and Maria over dinner. "It's an incredible opportunity," Daniel said, excitement and hesitation mingling in his voice. "But it would mean spending a lot of time abroad."

Emma and Maria exchanged glances, their expressions a mix of pride and concern. "It's a fantastic opportunity, Daniel," Maria said. "But what do you want?"

Daniel sighed, running a hand through his hair. "I love what we're doing here. But I also want to see what else is out there, to learn and grow."

Emma nodded thoughtfully. "Whatever you decide, we'll support you. You've always followed your heart, and it's led you to amazing places."

As Daniel contemplated his decision, Maria was dealing with her own exciting developments. The success of the community center had inspired other neighborhoods to start similar initiatives, and she found herself in demand as a consultant and speaker. She was passionate about expanding her reach, but it meant balancing her time and energy carefully.

One crisp autumn day, Maria received a call from a nonprofit organization in Los Angeles, interested in partnering with her to develop community centers on the West Coast. The idea of expanding her impact was exhilarating, but it also meant potentially spending long periods away from New York.

She shared her dilemma with Emma and Daniel as they walked through Central Park, the leaves crunching underfoot. "I want to help as many people as possible," Maria said. "But I also love being here, working with you both."

Emma smiled, linking arms with her friends. "We're all being pulled in different directions, but that doesn't mean we can't stay connected. We'll always be a team, no matter where we are."

As the trio faced these new opportunities, they realized that their journeys were evolving, leading them to explore new horizons while maintaining the bond that had brought them together. They decided to support one another's dreams, knowing that their friendship would remain the foundation of their success.

The winter holidays brought a sense of celebration and reflection. Daniel accepted the collaboration offer from the European firm, excited to bring his expertise to a new context. Emma's book was progressing well, with a tentative publication date set for the following year. Maria began working on plans for the West Coast community centers, coordinating with the nonprofit organization to create sustainable, impactful spaces.

On New Year's Eve, the trio gathered on the rooftop terrace, bundled in coats and scarves, sipping hot cocoa as they watched the fireworks light up the sky. The city sparkled below them, a testament to their shared dreams and the future that awaited them.

"To new beginnings," Emma said, raising her cup.

"To following our hearts," Daniel added.

"And to staying connected, no matter where we go," Maria finished.

As they toasted to the new year, they felt a sense of excitement and anticipation. They were ready to embrace the challenges and opportunities that lay ahead, confident in the strength of their friendship and the love they had for their city.

The future was bright, and their stories were far from over. Together, they would continue to explore, create, and inspire, their hearts forever intertwined with the heartbeat of New York.

CHAPTER 11

EMBRACING CHANGE

As winter settled over New York, the city seemed to take on a serene, almost magical quality. Snow blanketed the streets, and the hustle and bustle of the holiday season gave way to a quieter, more introspective time. For Emma, Daniel, and Maria, it was a period of preparation and reflection as they embraced the changes in their lives.

Emma's book project had entered its final stages. She spent long hours at her desk, surrounded by stacks of notes and photos. Isabella's artwork, now fully integrated into the manuscript, brought a vibrant, emotional depth to the stories Emma had curated. The book, tentatively titled "City Souls: Portraits of New York," was scheduled for release in the spring.

One snowy afternoon, as Emma worked on the final chapter, she received an unexpected phone call. It was from a major news network, interested in producing a documentary series based on her project. The idea of bringing "City Souls" to a broader audience thrilled Emma, but it also presented a new challenge: balancing the demands of book promotion with the intensive work required for the series.

That evening, she shared the news with Daniel and Maria over hot cocoa at Maria's café. "This is amazing, Emma!" Maria exclaimed. "You're going to reach so many more people."

Daniel nodded in agreement. "But it sounds like a lot of work. Are you ready for it?"

Emma smiled, though a hint of worry creased her brow. "I think so. It's just... a lot to juggle."

Maria reached out and squeezed Emma's hand. "We'll help however we can. You don't have to do it alone."

As Emma navigated the exciting yet demanding world of book publishing and television production, Daniel was preparing for his new adventure in Europe. He had accepted the collaboration offer and would be splitting his time between New York and various European cities. The project focused on revitalizing historic urban areas, blending modern sustainable design with preservation of cultural heritage.

One frosty morning, Daniel met with his team to finalize plans for his first trip abroad. They discussed project timelines, design concepts, and the logistics of managing an international collaboration. While the prospect of working in Europe was exhilarating, Daniel couldn't help but feel a pang of apprehension at the thought of being away from his friends and his city.

Before leaving, he organized a small farewell gathering at the construction site of the Brooklyn housing project. Emma, Maria, and their close friends joined him, sharing stories and laughter around a makeshift bonfire.

As they huddled together, Maria raised a toast. "To Daniel, and to new beginnings. We'll miss you, but we know you'll do incredible things."

Daniel smiled, feeling a deep sense of gratitude. "Thank you all. I'll be back often, and I promise to bring back plenty of stories."

Meanwhile, Maria was busy with her plans for the West Coast community centers. The nonprofit organization she was partnering with had secured locations in Los Angeles and San Francisco, and Maria was tasked with overseeing the initial planning and development stages. She made frequent trips to California, meeting with local leaders and community members to ensure the centers would meet their needs.

One sunny afternoon in Los Angeles, Maria stood in front of a vacant building that would soon be transformed into a bustling community hub. As she discussed renovation plans with her team, she felt a surge of excitement. This project was a testament to her dedication and passion for creating spaces where people could come together and thrive.

Back in New York, she continued to manage her cafés and the original community center, ensuring they remained vibrant, welcoming spaces. The balance between her commitments in New York and California was challenging, but Maria thrived on the energy and purpose it brought to her life.

As winter turned to spring, the trio found themselves adjusting to their new routines. Emma's book launch was a resounding success, with "City Souls" receiving rave reviews and quickly becoming a bestseller. The documentary series was in production, and Emma found herself in front of the camera, telling the stories she had so carefully curated.

Daniel settled into his transatlantic lifestyle, splitting his time between designing innovative urban spaces in Europe and overseeing projects back in New York. His work garnered international acclaim, and he was invited to speak at prestigious conferences and events.

Maria's community centers in California began to take shape, with the first center in Los Angeles opening its doors to enthusiastic community members. She divided her time between the coasts, ensuring each center was running smoothly and meeting its goals.

Despite their busy schedules and the physical distance between them, Emma, Daniel, and Maria remained as close as ever. They made time for regular video calls, sharing updates and offering support. They visited each other whenever possible, cherishing the moments they spent together in their beloved city.

One warm spring evening, the trio reunited in New York to celebrate the success of their individual ventures. They gathered on the rooftop terrace, the city skyline glittering in the background, and reflected on their journeys.

"We've come a long way," Emma said, her voice filled with pride. "And there's still so much more to do."

Daniel nodded. "We're just getting started."

Maria smiled, her heart full. "Together, we can do anything."

As they raised their glasses, they felt a profound sense of gratitude and anticipation. They had embraced change, faced challenges, and achieved incredible things. And they knew that, no matter where their paths led, their bond would remain unbreakable, their hearts forever connected to each other and to the city they loved.

CHAPTER 12

THE TEST OF TIME

Spring blossomed into summer, and New York City was alive with energy and activity. Emma, Daniel, and Maria had fully embraced their new paths, but as they balanced their individual projects and ambitions, they also faced new challenges that tested their resilience and commitment.

Emma's documentary series, "City Souls," premiered to critical acclaim. The series captured the essence of New York's diverse communities, and Emma quickly became a sought-after speaker at film festivals and community events. However, the demands of her growing fame began to weigh on her. The constant travel and public appearances left her feeling stretched thin, and she struggled to find time for herself.

One humid July afternoon, Emma found herself in a small hotel room in Los Angeles, exhausted after a day of interviews and press conferences. She stared at her reflection in the mirror, feeling a pang of loneliness. She missed the simplicity of her early days in New York, the quiet moments spent with friends and the comfort of familiar places.

Determined to regain her balance, Emma decided to take a short break and return to New York. She needed the city's grounding energy and the support of her friends to recharge. The moment she stepped off the plane and felt the city's vibrant pulse, she knew she had made the right decision.

Daniel, meanwhile, was thriving in his international collaborations. His work in Europe had earned him several prestigious awards, and his firm was expanding its global reach. Yet, despite his professional success, Daniel felt a growing sense of disconnection. The constant travel and time spent away from New York took a toll on him, and he missed the camaraderie and support of Emma and Maria.

One evening, as he looked out over the Paris skyline from his hotel room, Daniel felt a pang of homesickness. He realized that while his career was flourishing, his personal life was suffering. He longed for the simplicity of working on community projects in Brooklyn, the joy of collaborating with his friends, and the sense of purpose that came from being part of something larger than himself.

Determined to find a better balance, Daniel decided to return to New York more frequently, focusing on projects that allowed him to stay connected to the city and his friends.

Maria's community centers on the West Coast were thriving, but managing operations in two different regions proved challenging. She found herself constantly traveling between New York and California, and the pressure of maintaining her cafés and community initiatives began to wear on her. Despite her passion for her work, Maria felt overwhelmed and struggled to find time for herself.

One evening, as she sat in her Los Angeles apartment, Maria received a call from Emma. They talked for hours, sharing their struggles and offering each other support. Maria realized that she needed to delegate more responsibilities and trust her team to manage the day-to-day operations. This decision allowed her to focus on strategic planning and ensure she didn't lose herself in the process.

That summer, the trio decided to take a much-needed break and spend a weekend together in the Hamptons. The getaway was a chance to reconnect, recharge, and reflect on their journeys. They rented a charming beach house, spending their days lounging by the ocean, exploring local shops, and enjoying leisurely dinners under the stars.

One evening, as they sat around a bonfire on the beach, Emma shared her feelings of exhaustion and disconnection. "I've been running on empty, trying to keep up with everything," she admitted. "I miss the simplicity of our early days."

Daniel nodded in agreement. "I feel the same way. The constant travel and being away from New York has made me realize how much I value our time together and the work we do as a team."

Maria sighed, her eyes reflecting the flickering flames. "It's been tough balancing everything. But being here with you both, I feel grounded and inspired again."

They spent the weekend reminiscing about their past adventures and dreaming about future projects. The time away from the city allowed them to gain perspective and renew their commitment to their individual and collective goals.

As they returned to New York, they felt a renewed sense of purpose and clarity. Emma decided to scale back on her public appearances, focusing instead on projects that allowed her to stay connected to her roots. Daniel restructured his work to spend more time in New York, balancing his international commitments with local projects that brought him joy. Maria delegated more responsibilities to her team, ensuring she had time to nurture her well-being and creativity.

Together, they continued to support each other, navigating the challenges and triumphs of their evolving lives. The city, with its ever-changing landscape and endless possibilities, remained their anchor and inspiration.

As the summer turned to autumn, the trio stood on the rooftop terrace, looking out over the city they loved. They knew that no matter what challenges lay ahead, their friendship and shared vision would guide them through.

"To us," Emma said, raising her glass. "And to New York, our forever home."

Daniel and Maria clinked their glasses with hers, their hearts full of gratitude and hope.

"To us," they echoed, knowing that together, they could overcome anything.

CHAPTER 13

THE POWER OF CONNECTION

Autumn in New York City brought a fresh wave of inspiration to Emma, Daniel, and Maria. With their renewed sense of purpose, they threw themselves into their work, each of them more mindful of balancing their professional ambitions with personal well-being.

Emma, now back in New York full-time, focused on new projects that allowed her to stay connected to the city and its people. She started a new multimedia series, "Hidden Gems," exploring lesser-known stories and unsung heroes of New York. This project not only reignited her passion but also allowed her to work at a pace that was sustainable and fulfilling.

One crisp October morning, Emma visited a small, family-owned bookstore in Harlem to interview its owner,

Mr. Jameson, an elderly gentleman who had dedicated his life to promoting literacy and community engagement. As Emma listened to his stories, she felt a deep sense of gratitude for the opportunity to highlight such impactful individuals.

Later that day, she met Daniel and Maria for coffee at their favorite spot in the Village. The café's cozy interior and the comforting aroma of freshly brewed coffee provided the perfect setting for their catch-up session.

"I love your new series idea," Daniel said, taking a sip of his coffee. "It's exactly what we need right now – focusing on the positive and the people who make a difference."

Emma smiled. "It's been incredibly rewarding. And it feels good to be working on something that's not only meaningful but also manageable."

Maria nodded in agreement. "Speaking of meaningful projects, I've been thinking about expanding the community center's programs to include more arts and culture events. We've seen such a positive response from the community, and I think we can do even more."

Emma's eyes lit up. "That sounds fantastic! I'd love to help out with that. Maybe we could feature some of the people from 'Hidden Gems' in the events."

"That's a great idea," Daniel said. "And speaking of community, I've been thinking about starting a mentorship program for young architects. There's so much talent in this city, and I want to give back by helping the next generation."

Maria beamed. "I love that. It's all about connection, isn't it? Whether it's through stories, art, or mentorship, we're creating a network of support and inspiration."

As the trio continued to brainstorm and share ideas, they realized the power of their collective efforts. By working together and supporting each other, they could create a ripple effect of positive change throughout the city.

In the following weeks, their plans began to take shape. Emma's "Hidden Gems" series gained traction, attracting a dedicated following of viewers who were inspired by the stories she shared. She collaborated with Maria to organize a series of events at the community center, featuring live readings, art exhibitions, and performances by local artists.

Daniel's mentorship program quickly became a success. He partnered with local schools and community organizations to offer workshops and internships to aspiring young architects. The program provided invaluable opportunities for students to learn from professionals and gain hands-on experience in the field.

One brisk November evening, the trio hosted their first collaborative event at Maria's community center. The space was filled with artwork, photographs, and installations that celebrated the diverse stories of New York's hidden gems. The air buzzed with excitement as community members mingled, shared stories, and connected with one another.

Emma took the stage to introduce the evening's program, her heart swelling with pride and gratitude. "Thank you all for being here tonight," she began. "This event is a celebration of the incredible people and stories that make New York City so special. It's about recognizing the power of connection and the impact we can have when we come together as a community."

The evening was a resounding success. Attendees left feeling inspired and uplifted, their hearts full of new stories and connections. For Emma, Daniel, and Maria, the event was a powerful reminder of why they had embarked on their respective journeys in the first place – to make a difference, to uplift others, and to build a stronger, more connected community.

As the year drew to a close, the trio continued to find new ways to collaborate and support each other. They knew that the power of their connection, both with each other and with the wider community, was the key to their success and fulfillment.

One snowy December night, they gathered once again on the rooftop terrace, the city lights twinkling below them. They toasted to the year that had passed and the adventures that lay ahead, their hearts full of hope and determination.

"To connection," Emma said, raising her glass.

"To making a difference," Daniel added.

"And to the incredible journey ahead," Maria finished.

As they clinked their glasses, they felt a deep sense of gratitude for the paths they had chosen and the bond that had brought them together. They knew that whatever challenges or opportunities the future held, they would face them together, their hearts forever intertwined with the heartbeat of New York.

CHAPTER 14

SEASONS OF CHANGE

The new year ushered in a season of change and growth for Emma, Daniel, and Maria. As winter transitioned to spring, each of them found themselves embarking on new adventures while remaining deeply connected to their beloved city and each other.

Emma's "Hidden Gems" series continued to thrive, drawing even more attention and accolades. She received an invitation to speak at a major media conference, where she would present her work and discuss the importance of community-focused storytelling. The opportunity excited and intimidated her, but with the encouragement of her friends, she prepared diligently.

The day of the conference arrived, and Emma stood backstage, her heart racing. She thought of the countless stories she had encountered and the people who had inspired her. Taking a deep breath, she stepped onto the stage, greeted by a warm round of applause.

"Thank you for being here," Emma began, her voice steady and clear. "The stories we tell have the power to shape our understanding of the world and each other. Through 'Hidden Gems,' I've had the privilege of uncovering the extraordinary lives of ordinary people. It's a reminder that everyone has a story worth telling and that we're all connected by our shared humanity."

Her presentation was met with enthusiastic applause and sparked meaningful conversations about the role of media in fostering community and empathy. Emma felt a renewed sense of purpose, knowing her work was making a difference.

Meanwhile, Daniel's mentorship program had flourished, and he was now working on a new project in New York that combined his love for architecture with his commitment to sustainability. Partnering with local government and environmental organizations, he embarked on an ambitious plan to transform an abandoned industrial area into a vibrant, eco-friendly community space.

The project involved repurposing old warehouses into green housing, creating urban gardens, and developing public spaces that encouraged social interaction and environmental awareness. Daniel's vision was to create a model for sustainable urban living that could be replicated in other cities.

One afternoon, as he walked through the construction site with his team, Daniel felt a sense of fulfillment. He was not only building structures but also fostering a community that valued sustainability and connection. The project garnered attention from urban planners and environmentalists, further solidifying Daniel's reputation as a forward-thinking architect.

Maria, too, was in the midst of significant changes. The success of her community centers on both coasts inspired her to expand her efforts. She launched a new initiative called "Art for All," a program that brought art and cultural activities to underserved communities. The program aimed to provide creative outlets and foster a sense of belonging and expression.

Working closely with artists, educators, and local leaders, Maria organized workshops, exhibitions, and performances that celebrated diverse voices and talents. The initiative was met with enthusiasm and gratitude from the communities it served, reaffirming Maria's belief in the transformative power of art.

One evening, Maria hosted an "Art for All" event at the community center in Brooklyn. The space was filled with vibrant artworks, music, and the laughter of children participating in art activities. Emma and Daniel were there, marveling at the energy and creativity that filled the room.

As they watched a group of children proudly displaying their paintings, Maria turned to her friends with a smile. "This is what it's all about," she said. "Creating spaces where people can express themselves and connect with each other."

Emma nodded. "It's beautiful, Maria. You're making such a difference."

Daniel agreed. "Seeing these kids so happy and engaged—it's inspiring. You're giving them something invaluable."

Spring blossomed into summer, and the trio continued to support each other through their individual journeys. They made time for regular get-togethers, whether it was a leisurely brunch, a visit to a new art exhibit, or a simple walk through Central Park. These moments of connection were vital, grounding them amid their busy lives.

One balmy June evening, they gathered on the rooftop terrace, enjoying the warm breeze and the spectacular view of the city skyline. The past year had been one of growth and change, but their bond remained as strong as ever.

"To us," Emma said, raising her glass. "And to the incredible things we've accomplished."

"To the power of community," Daniel added, clinking his glass with theirs.

"And to the adventures yet to come," Maria finished, her eyes sparkling with excitement.

As they toasted to their shared journey, they felt a deep sense of gratitude and anticipation. The seasons of change had brought them closer together, each step forward a testament to their resilience, creativity, and the unbreakable bond they shared with each other and with New York.

CHAPTER 15

NEW HORIZONS

As summer enveloped New York in its warm embrace, Emma, Daniel, and Maria found themselves at the cusp of new horizons, both in their personal and professional lives. Each had grown in ways they hadn't anticipated, and their shared journey had equipped them with the strength and inspiration to face whatever lay ahead.

Emma's "Hidden Gems" series had not only gained national acclaim but also attracted the attention of international media. She received an offer to create a similar series in cities around the world, showcasing the hidden stories and unsung heroes of diverse cultures. The opportunity was thrilling, yet daunting. It meant extended travel and time away from New York, the city that had become her creative anchor.

Over dinner one evening, Emma shared her news with Daniel and Maria. "I've been offered a chance to take 'Hidden Gems' global," she said, excitement and apprehension mingling in her voice. "It's a dream come true, but I'm not sure I'm ready to leave New York for so long."

Daniel and Maria exchanged glances, their faces lighting up with pride and understanding. "Emma, this is incredible," Maria said. "Your work has always been about connecting people and telling their stories. Imagine the impact you could have on a global scale."

Daniel nodded. "We'll miss you, of course, but this is an amazing opportunity. You've always embraced change and challenges. This is just another step in your journey."

Emma smiled, her heart swelling with gratitude. "I guess I'm just afraid of losing my connection to home, to you both."

"You'll always have us," Daniel said. "And New York will always be here, waiting for your return."

With their support, Emma decided to embark on the new venture, excited about the stories she would uncover and the connections she would make across the world. She promised to stay in touch and visit as often as she could, knowing that her friends and her city would remain her foundation.

Daniel, inspired by Emma's courage, began to explore new horizons in his own career. His sustainable community project in New York had garnered international interest, leading to invitations to speak at conferences and consult on similar projects in other cities. He decided to take on a new challenge: developing a global network of eco-friendly urban spaces that promoted sustainable living and community engagement.

While this meant more travel for Daniel as well, he felt invigorated by the possibility of making a broader impact. He envisioned a future where cities around the world could learn from New York's example, creating environments that were not only sustainable but also deeply connected to their communities.

Maria, too, found herself at a crossroads. Her "Art for All" initiative had grown beyond her wildest dreams, with requests to expand the program to other states and even countries. She realized that to truly scale the impact of her work, she needed to build a robust framework that could be implemented globally. This meant establishing partnerships, training local leaders, and creating a sustainable model that could be adapted to different cultural contexts.

One sunny afternoon, as they sat in a park discussing their plans, Maria shared her vision. "I want 'Art for All' to be a movement, something that transcends borders and brings people together through creativity. But it's going to require a lot of work and travel."

Emma reached out and squeezed Maria's hand. "You've always been a pioneer, Maria. Your passion and dedication will inspire countless others. We're here for you, no matter where your journey takes you."

Daniel added, "And remember, we're all expanding our horizons. This isn't the end of our story – it's just the beginning of a new chapter."

As summer turned to fall, the trio prepared for their respective adventures. They threw a grand farewell party on the rooftop terrace, inviting friends and colleagues who had been part of their journey. The evening was filled with laughter, memories, and heartfelt toasts.

"To new horizons," Emma said, raising her glass. "And to the unbreakable bond that ties us together, no matter where we are in the world."

"To the power of our dreams," Daniel added. "And the impact we can make when we follow our passions."

"And to the journey ahead," Maria finished, her eyes shining with determination. "Together, we've accomplished so much. Imagine what we can do next."

As the sun set over the city, painting the sky in hues of pink and gold, Emma, Daniel, and Maria stood arm in arm, their hearts full of hope and excitement. They knew that while their paths might diverge, their friendship and their love for New York would always bring them back together.

The seasons of their lives had brought change and growth, but through it all, they had remained steadfast in their support for each other. They were ready to embrace the future, knowing that their shared journey had only just begun.

CHAPTER 16

ROOTS AND WINGS

With their farewells exchanged and plans set in motion, Emma, Daniel, and Maria embarked on their new adventures. Yet, even as they spread their wings to explore new horizons, the roots they had planted in New York kept them grounded.

Emma's global venture with "Hidden Gems" took her to cities around the world. From the bustling streets of Tokyo to the historic alleys of Rome, she uncovered stories of resilience, creativity, and community spirit. Her journey was a whirlwind of discovery and inspiration, but she made it a point to return to New York regularly. Each visit recharged her, reconnecting her with the city's vibrant energy and the people who had become her family.

During one of her trips back, Emma organized a special screening of the latest episodes of "Hidden Gems" at the community center. Daniel and Maria, along with many of their friends, attended the event. The room was filled with excitement as the lights dimmed and the screen came to life, showcasing the incredible stories Emma had gathered from around the world.

After the screening, Emma took the stage to a standing ovation. "Thank you all for being here," she said, her voice filled with emotion. "This journey has been incredible, but it's your support and the love I have for this city that keep me going. New York is my home, and it always will be."

Daniel's work on sustainable urban spaces also took him across the globe. He spent months in cities like Copenhagen and Melbourne, collaborating with local architects and city planners to create eco-friendly, community-centric developments. His projects received widespread acclaim, and Daniel found immense satisfaction in knowing that his work was making a difference on a global scale.

However, he never lost sight of his roots. Whenever he returned to New York, he spent time mentoring young architects and overseeing the ongoing development of his project in Brooklyn. One evening, he hosted a workshop at his alma mater, sharing his experiences and insights with aspiring architects. The room buzzed with enthusiasm as students engaged in lively discussions about sustainability and innovation.

"It's not just about building structures," Daniel told them. "It's about creating spaces that foster community and connection. That's what I've learned from New York, and it's a lesson I carry with me wherever I go."

Maria's "Art for All" initiative expanded to new heights, with programs launching in cities from London to Mumbai. She traveled extensively to set up these new branches, training local leaders and ensuring that each program was tailored to its community. Her efforts were met with overwhelming support, and Maria found herself at the forefront of a global movement that celebrated creativity and inclusivity.

Yet, like her friends, Maria remained deeply connected to New York. She continued to host events at the community center and spent time with the artists and residents who had been her initial inspiration. One sunny afternoon, she organized an outdoor art festival in Brooklyn, bringing together artists from around the world to share their work and engage with the community.

As Maria walked through the festival, admiring the colorful displays and listening to the laughter and chatter around her, she felt a profound sense of fulfillment. "This is why I do what I do," she thought. "To bring people together, to create beauty and connection."

The trio's regular reunions became a cherished tradition. They made it a point to gather every few months, whether in New York or in one of the cities they were working in. These reunions were a time for reflection, celebration, and planning for the future.

One autumn evening, they found themselves back on the rooftop terrace, the city lights twinkling below them. They shared stories of their travels and the people they had met, their laughter mingling with the cool night air.

"It's amazing how much we've accomplished," Emma said, gazing out at the skyline. "But it's even more incredible that through it all, we've stayed connected."

Daniel nodded. "Our roots are here, in New York, but our wings have taken us to places we never imagined. It's the best of both worlds."

Maria raised her glass. "To roots and wings," she said, her eyes shining with pride and love. "And to the journey that continues to unfold."

They clinked their glasses, their hearts full of gratitude for the paths they had taken and the bond that held them together. No matter where their adventures led them, they knew they could always count on each other and the city that had shaped their lives.

CHAPTER 17

UNEXPECTED CHALLENGES

As the leaves began to change and the air grew crisp, Emma, Daniel, and Maria found themselves facing new and unexpected challenges that tested their resilience and adaptability.

Emma was in Paris, working on a "Hidden Gems" episode focused on the city's vibrant immigrant communities. She was deep in a fascinating interview with a Syrian refugee who had become a celebrated chef, sharing his story of struggle and triumph. Suddenly, her phone buzzed with an urgent message from her producer back in New York. There was a technical glitch with the latest episode, and the network was considering pulling it if the issue wasn't resolved quickly.

Panicking, Emma wrapped up the interview and rushed back to her hotel, trying to troubleshoot the problem remotely. Despite her best efforts, she realized she needed her team in New York to handle it. She made a frantic call to her producer, who assured her they would do everything possible to fix the issue.

Feeling helpless so far from home, Emma decided to fly back to New York to personally oversee the resolution. The next few days were a blur of meetings, phone calls, and late nights at the editing suite. Finally, just hours before the episode was set to air, the problem was fixed, and the show went on as scheduled.

Exhausted but relieved, Emma took a moment to reflect on the experience. "I guess this is the reality of pursuing your dreams," she thought. "There will always be challenges, but it's how you face them that matters."

Meanwhile, Daniel was in Singapore, working on a groundbreaking project to create a floating eco-city. The innovative design aimed to address space constraints and rising sea levels, making it one of his most ambitious projects yet. However, he faced significant pushback from local authorities who were skeptical of the feasibility and cost of such a venture.

Determined to prove the value of his vision, Daniel organized a series of presentations and workshops to demonstrate the potential benefits of the floating city. He brought in experts from various fields to support his case and engaged the local community in discussions about the project's long-term impact.

Despite his efforts, progress was slow, and Daniel began to doubt whether he could overcome the bureaucratic hurdles. One evening, he called Maria, seeking her advice and support.

"Maria, I'm hitting a wall here," he admitted. "No matter what I do, it feels like I'm not making any headway."

Maria listened patiently, her voice calm and reassuring. "Daniel, every great project faces resistance at some point. You've always been a visionary, and it's natural for people to be cautious about something so new and bold. Keep pushing, keep believing in your vision. You'll find a way."

Inspired by her words, Daniel redoubled his efforts, eventually gaining the support he needed to move forward. The project still had a long way to go, but Daniel felt a renewed sense of purpose and determination.

Back in New York, Maria was dealing with her own set of challenges. The expansion of "Art for All" had stretched her resources thin, and she struggled to maintain the quality and impact of the programs. Additionally, a major donor had unexpectedly pulled out, leaving a significant gap in funding.

Maria spent countless hours brainstorming solutions, reaching out to potential new donors, and rallying her team. Despite the setbacks, she remained committed to her vision, knowing how much the programs meant to the communities they served.

One evening, as she was working late at the community center, Emma and Daniel surprised her with a visit. They brought coffee and pastries, insisting she take a break to talk and relax.

"We've all been facing challenges lately," Emma said, taking a sip of her coffee. "But we're here for each other, no matter what."

Daniel nodded in agreement. "You've done amazing things, Maria. We're going to help you through this."

Their support and encouragement gave Maria the boost she needed. With renewed energy, she tackled the funding issue, organizing a successful fundraising gala that not only filled the financial gap but also raised awareness about the importance of arts in underserved communities.

As the season drew to a close, the trio reflected on the challenges they had faced and the strength they had found in their friendship. They realized that while their paths were not always easy, their shared journey provided the support and inspiration they needed to overcome any obstacle.

On a chilly November night, they gathered once more on the rooftop terrace, the city below a tapestry of lights. They toasted to their resilience and the unbreakable bond that had carried them through yet another chapter of their lives.

"To facing challenges head-on," Emma said, raising her glass.

"To believing in our visions," Daniel added.

"And to the power of friendship," Maria finished, her heart full of gratitude.

As they clinked their glasses, they knew that no matter what challenges lay ahead, they would face them together,

drawing strength from their shared experiences and the city
that had always been their home.

CHAPTER 18

SERENDIPITOUS ENCOUNTERS

Winter settled over New York with a blanket of snow, turning the city into a sparkling wonderland. Despite the cold, Emma, Daniel, and Maria continued to pursue their passions with the same fervor that had always driven them. This season, however, brought unexpected encounters that would further shape their journeys.

Emma was back in New York for a brief respite from her global travels. One frosty morning, she decided to visit her favorite café in the West Village. As she sipped her coffee and reviewed her latest notes, a familiar face walked in. It was Jack, a fellow journalist she had met years ago during a conference in Los Angeles.

"Emma? Is that you?" Jack asked, surprised but delighted.

"Jack! What are you doing here?" Emma replied, equally astonished.

They quickly fell into an animated conversation, catching up on each other's lives and careers. Jack was now a senior correspondent for a major news network and had recently moved to New York. He shared his admiration for Emma's "Hidden Gems" series, which he had followed avidly.

As they talked, Emma felt a spark of inspiration. She proposed a collaboration: a special feature that combined her in-depth community stories with his broad investigative reporting. Jack was intrigued by the idea, and they decided to explore it further. This serendipitous encounter opened new doors for Emma, blending her passion for storytelling with a fresh, collaborative approach.

Daniel's project in Singapore was progressing, albeit slowly. During a break from his intense schedule, he visited a local art exhibition showcasing eco-friendly design. There, he met Aisha, a renowned environmental artist whose work focused on integrating natural elements into urban spaces. Intrigued by her innovative approach, Daniel struck up a conversation.

They quickly discovered a shared vision of sustainable urban living. Aisha's artistic perspective added a new dimension to Daniel's architectural designs. She proposed an art installation for his floating city project, using recycled materials to create a living sculpture that would symbolize harmony between nature and urban life.

Daniel was captivated by the idea and invited Aisha to collaborate on the project. This partnership not only enriched his work but also provided him with a renewed sense of creativity and purpose. Together, they began to transform the floating city into a living, breathing work of art.

Maria, busy expanding "Art for All," found herself in an unexpected encounter during a fundraising event in London. Among the attendees was Gabriel, a philanthropist with a deep passion for the arts. He was impressed by Maria's vision and dedication and offered significant financial support for the initiative.

Gabriel's involvement went beyond funding. He brought a wealth of experience in nonprofit management and offered to help Maria streamline operations and expand her reach. With his guidance, Maria was able to set up new programs more efficiently and connect with a broader network of artists and supporters.

One snowy evening, back in New York, the trio reunited at a cozy jazz club in Harlem. They shared stories of their unexpected encounters and the new opportunities that had come their way.

"Life has a funny way of bringing people together at just the right moment," Emma mused, her eyes twinkling with excitement about her collaboration with Jack.

"It's amazing how these chance meetings can open up new paths," Daniel agreed. "Meeting Aisha has given me a whole new perspective on integrating art and architecture."

"And Gabriel has been a game-changer for 'Art for All,'" Maria added. "His support and expertise are helping us reach more communities than ever before."

As the music played softly in the background, they toasted to the serendipitous encounters that had enriched their lives. They knew that while their journeys were far from predictable, it was these unexpected moments that added depth and excitement to their adventures.

With winter in full swing, they embraced the warmth of their friendship and the opportunities that lay ahead, ready to face whatever the new year would bring.

NY Forever

www.ingramcontent.com/pod-product-compliance
Lightning Source LLC
Chambersburg PA
CBHW061327120726
48001CB00002B/725